# Growing Patterns

Fibonacci Numbers in Nature

## Sarah C. Campbell

Photographs by
Sarah C. Campbell
and Richard P. Campbell

ASTRA YOUNG READERS

AN IMPRINT OF ASTRA BOOKS FOR YOUNG READERS

New York

For Graeme, Nathan, and Douglas

Text copyright © 2010 by Sarah C. Campbell
Photographs copyright © 2010 by Sarah C. Campbell and Richard P. Campbell

For information about permission to reproduce selections from this book, please contact permissions@astrapublishinghouse.com.

Astra Young Readers
An imprint of Astra Books for Young Readers, a division of Astra Publishing House
astrapublishinghouse.com
Printed in China

Library of Congress Cataloging-in-Publication Data

Campbell, Sarah C.
  Growing patterns : fibonacci numbers in nature / Sarah C. Campbell ; photographs by Sarah C. Campbell and Richard P. Campbell.
    p. cm.
  ISBN: 978-1-59078-752-6 (hardcover : alk. paper)
  1. Fibonacci numbers—Juvenile literature. 2. Mathematics in nature—Juvenile literature.  I. Campbell, Richard P., ill. II. Title.
  QA246.5.C36 2010
  512.7'2—dc22
                    2009024075

ISBN: 978-1-63592-837-2 (pb)
ISBN: 978-1-63592-489-3 (eBook)

First paperback edition, 2022

10 9 8 7 6 5 4 3 2 1

The text of this book is set in Minion.

## Acknowledgments

The inspiration for a book may happen in a moment—in this case, it was during a portfolio critique with an art director at an SCBWI conference. The making of a book, however, is a long and collaborative process. I had help along the way from many people.

First, I thank Richard, my partner in life and in creative pursuits. I appreciate your interest, support, advice, technical expertise, and artistic eye.

I thank my editor, Andy Boyles, for his deft hand with explanatory prose for young readers. For reviewing the manuscript, I thank Dr. Pau Atela, professor of mathematics at Smith College in Northampton, Massachusetts; Dr. Connie Campbell, professor of mathematics at Millsaps College in Jackson, Mississippi; and Dr. Matthew Bardoe, mathematics teacher at Latin School of Chicago. I thank my parents, Dave and Patty Crosby, for creating a homeplace perfect for photographing wildflowers, for lending me the books to identify them, and for reading many drafts. I thank my aunt Kathy Welde, who gave us the nautilus shell.

Finally, I thank the young people who read drafts along the way and gave me invaluable feedback: Susanna and Charley Blount, Sophia Bowley, and Mary Emerson Owen. I also thank Beth West's second-grade class at Davis Magnet School in Jackson, Mississippi, especially Ruben Banks and Bryce Winn, who together wrote a full page of comments.
                                                                    —SCC

A seed grows into a plant.
When it is all grown up, it might be
a tuft of grass, a daisy, or a tree.
The seed has built-in instructions for how
the plant will grow.
What shape will it be?
What size?
What color?

This peace lily has white flowers—
always with one petal.
The number of petals on a flower and the
shapes and patterns they make come from
two things: the plant's instructions and its
growing conditions.

This is a crown of thorns.
Count the petals.

This is a spiderwort.
Count the petals.

This is a flowering quince.
Count the petals.

This is a cosmos.
Count the petals.

The numbers of petals on these flowers—1, 2, 3, 5, and 8—have a special relationship to one another and to nature.

Just like this story,
which started with one seed and a flower with one petal,
this special pattern begins with 1 and 1.
To get the next number, you add 1 plus 1, which equals 2.

1 + 1 = 2

This is the rule for these special numbers:
in order to get the next number,
you add the two numbers before it.
So, the number after 2 is:
1 plus 2, which equals 3.

The next number is:
2 plus 3, which equals 5.

2 + 3 = 5

The next number is: 3 plus 5, which equals 8.

People first wrote about these special numbers in ancient India. But today the numbers are named after an Italian mathematician. He was called Fibonacci (fib-uh-**notch**-ee). Over the years, people have noticed that Fibonacci numbers are everywhere in nature. Here are more flowers with numbers of petals that equal Fibonacci numbers.

The numbers go higher and higher,
always following the same rule.
The number after 8 is:
5 plus 8, which equals 13.

1 + 1 = 2
1 + 2 = 3
2 + 3 = 5
3 + 5 = 8
5 + 8 = 13
8 + 13 = 21
13 + 21 = 34

13

5 + 8 = 13

The first 12 numbers in the Fibonacci sequence are 1, 1, 2, 3, 5, 8, 13, 21, 34, 55, 89, and 144.

So far, each of the flowers in these pictures has had one Fibonacci number: the number of petals. In pinecones, sunflowers, and pineapples, there are even more Fibonacci numbers.

The bracts growing on the bottom of a pinecone look like petals, but each has a sharp tip. Ouch! They grow out from the stem in spirals.

All the pictures on these two pages show the same pinecone. On the next page, some of the spirals were printed darker to help you see the pattern.

Count the spirals. Counting the spirals that go one way (in the photo above), this pinecone has 8. Counting the spirals that go the other way (in the photo on the left), it has 13. These are both Fibonacci numbers.

Look at the disk flowers in the center of this sunflower. They grow in spirals, too. Can you count the spirals?

Like the pinecone, the sunflower makes two kinds of spirals. One curves in one direction. The other goes in the opposite direction.

When Fibonacci numbers show up in spirals, the numbers are always next to each other in the pattern.

1, 1, 2, 3, 5, 8, 13, 21, **34**, **55**, 89, 144 . . .

The sections on the outside of a pineapple grow in spirals. You would be able to count the spirals going in three directions—if you could turn the pineapple as you counted.

On the next page, in the photo on the bottom right, you would find 5 spirals. At the top right, 8 spirals. In the photo on the left, 13.

Fibonacci!

**13**

**8**

**5**

Look at a real pineapple to count all of the spirals.

The third way we see Fibonacci numbers in nature is in a different kind of spiral. This time it is on an animal. This spiral starts at the beginning of the Fibonacci sequence and grows the same way the Fibonacci numbers grow. Look at the drawing on the next page. The spiral starts in a corner of the red square, curves through the orange square, the yellow square, the green square, the blue square, and the purple square.

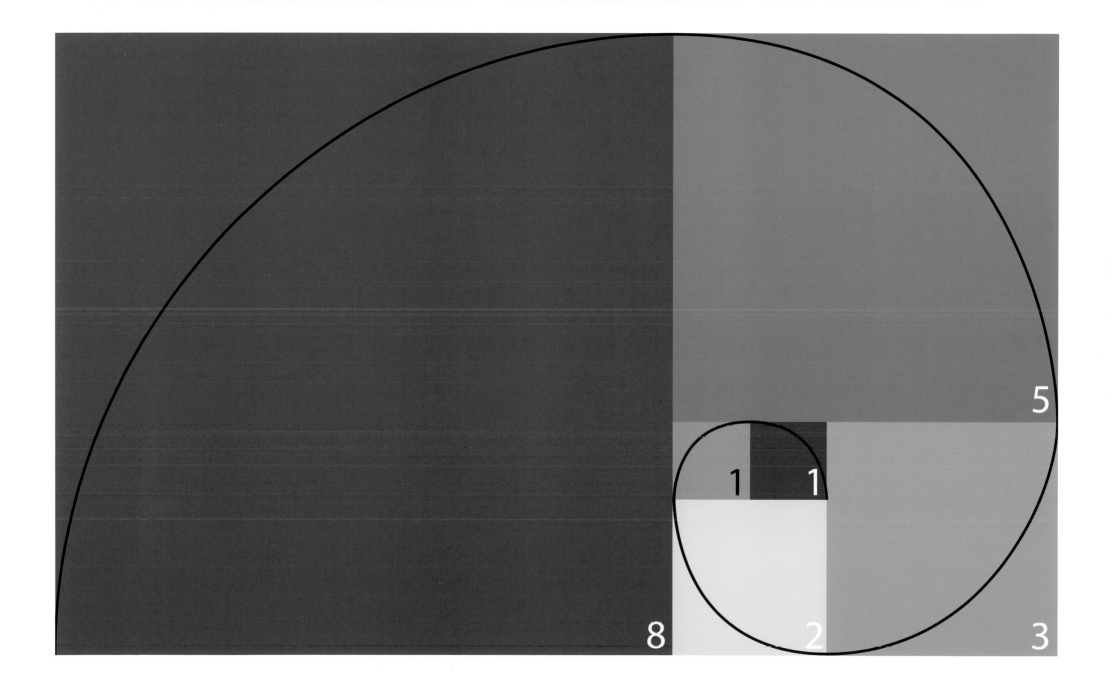

This spiral is like the one that is formed by a nautilus as it grows. The nautilus is a sea animal, and its shell is similar to a snail's. Just like plants, animals have built-in instructions that determine how they grow. The photograph on the next page shows the inside of an empty nautilus shell.

Do you see the spiral?

Not all numbers in nature are Fibonacci numbers. A dogwood has 4 petals, and an amaryllis has 6. The garden snail and the fiddlehead on the fern are spirals, but they don't have the same shape as the nautilus. The next time you are outside, take a close look at the plants and animals. See if you can find Fibonacci numbers, spirals, or some other pattern. They are growing all around.

# More About Fibonacci Numbers

### Fibonacci, the Man
The mathematician who first wrote about Fibonacci numbers was an Italian named Leonardo. He lived in Pisa, so his name was Leonardo of Pisa. When he completed his most important book, *Liber Abaci*, in 1202, he signed his name Fibonacci, which can be translated as "son of Bonaccio." Fibonacci is how he is most commonly known.

### Before Fibonacci
The interesting properties of this special set of numbers {1, 1, 2, 3, 5, 8, 13, . . .}were known to scholars in India before Fibonacci's time. These scholars included Pingala, Virhanka, Gopala, and Hemachandra.

### The Rabbit Problem
Fibonacci first described his famous number sequence as the solution to a math problem about how rabbit families grow each time another rabbit in the family has babies. However, the number of babies that real rabbits have has nothing to do with the Fibonacci pattern.

### Why Fibonacci Numbers?
Scientists who study plants have found that Fibonacci numbers show up often in plants that have multiple parts (such as leaves, petals, or seeds) arranged around a single stem. A study found that two successive Fibonacci numbers appeared in more than 90 percent of such plants. The frequent appearance of Fibonacci numbers in nature has been a puzzle for a long time. Recently, scientists and mathematicians have been able to reproduce the patterns in laboratory studies and have offered new ideas about why the numbers arise.

### The Golden Ratio
If you divide any number (except for the first few) from the Fibonacci sequence by the number immediately before it—for example 21 ÷ 13 or 55 ÷ 34—you get a number that is close to the "golden ratio," which is 1.61803. The golden ratio goes back even further in history than Fibonacci numbers. It was used in ancient buildings and written about in the earliest-known books about geometry and math. The pages you are reading are 12 inches wide and 7.4 inches tall, which makes them close to golden rectangles: 12 ÷ 7.4 = 1.62. If they were 7.41643 inches tall, they would be *perfect* golden rectangles.

### Lucas Numbers
Another sequence of numbers, which operates just like Fibonacci numbers, also appears in nature. The only difference is the starting numbers. Named after the French mathematician Édouard Lucas, this sequence starts with 2 and 1. Then, it follows this rule: to get each successive number, you add the two before it. So, 2, 1, 3, 4, 7, 11, 18, 29, 47 . . .

### Golden Spiral
This diagram shows a true golden spiral. It is similar to, but not exactly like, the diagram on page 27, which comes from the Fibonacci pattern. A true golden spiral becomes wider as it grows by a factor of the golden ratio, or 1.61803, in the course of each quarter turn.

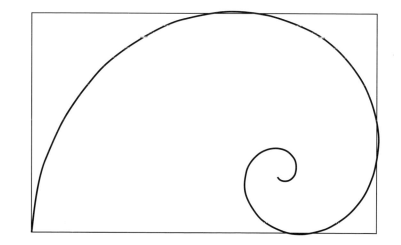

## Glossary

**bract** a leaflike or scalelike plant part, usually small.

**disk flowers** a group of small flowers that makes up part of a composite flower, typically found in the center of the head, as with a sunflower.

**Fibonacci numbers** the sequence of numbers—1, 1, 2, 3, 5, 8, 13, 21 . . .—in which each successive number is equal to the sum of the two preceding numbers.

**golden ratio** the irrational number $(1 + \sqrt{5})/2$, or approximately 1.61803.

**golden rectangle** a rectangle in which the longer sides are 1.61803 times the length of the shorter sides. The ancient Greeks believed that a rectangle built to this ratio was the most pleasing to the eye.

**instructions** detailed directions on procedures to follow.

**pattern** a design, with consistent characteristic form, of natural or accidental origin.

**petal** a part of a flower, usually showy and colored.

**seed** a fertilized plant ovule containing an embryo capable of developing a new plant.

**sequence** a series of objects or symbols that follow one after another in a set order.

**spiral** the path of a point moving around a fixed center at an increasing or decreasing distance.

Spirals

Butterweed

A. Lyre-Leaved Sage
B. Calla Lily
C. Crown of Thorns
D. Trillium
E. Vinca
F. Cosmos